STEVEN WEINBERG

GLORY AND TERROR

THE GROWING NUCLEAR DANGER

PREFACE BY ANTHONY LEWIS

as published in The New York Review of Books

NEW YORK REVIEW BOOKS, NEW YORK

THIS IS A NEW YORK REVIEW BOOK

PUBLISHED BY THE NEW YORK REVIEW OF BOOKS

GLORY AND TERROR: THE GROWING NUCLEAR DANGER
by Steven Weinberg

This edition published in 2004 in the United States of America by
The New York Review of Books, 1755 Broadway, New York, NY 10019
www.nybooks.com

Book and cover design by Milton Glaser, Inc.

Library of Congress Cataloging-in-Publication Data
Weinberg, Steven.
Glory and terror : the growing nuclear danger / Steven Weinberg ; introduction by
Anthony Lewis.
p. cm.
Includes bibliographical references.
ISBN 1-59017-130-6 (pbk. : alk. paper)
1. Nuclear weapons--United States. 2. United States—Military policy. 3. Ballistic missile
defenses—United States. 4. United States—Politics and government—2001– I. Title.
UA23.W36963 2004
355.8'25119'0973—dc22

2004010495

ISBN 1-59017-130-6

Printed in the United States of America on acid-free paper.

July 2004

1 3 5 7 9 10 8 6 4 2

CONTENTS

PREFACE

AT THE HEIGHT OF THE COLD WAR THE AMERICAN public feared that what was called the balance of terror—the assurance of devastating retaliation if either the Soviet Union or the US used nuclear weapons against the other—would not hold. Nelson Rockefeller urged us to build bomb shelters. During the Cuban missile crisis of 1962, which was as close as we came to the use of nuclear weapons, a friend of mine in Washington, the wife of a high official, had what she called her "flee bag": supplies to take with her to the hills if Armageddon came.

Today the fear is of a very different kind: that nuclear weapons may be acquired, and used, not by a powerful state but by a rogue nation or gang of terrorists unconcerned about its own destruction by a retaliatory strike, indeed willing to die for an ideological or religious cause. The fear is less focused than ours was during the missile crisis. But it is all around us, lurking, rising in our minds when a mass terrorist outrage takes place in Bali or Spain. We know that we could not have a balance of terror with minds impervious to reason and humanity.

In the face of this profound threat, the United States government is planning to cut back what it spends to work with Russia on reducing the menace of nuclear weapons. It is not doing nearly all it could to discover what regimes and, possibly, terrorist groups were instructed in nuclear weaponry by Abdul Qadeer Khan, the disgraced leader of Pakistan's nuclear program—disgraced but protected.

Where the United States is making a crash effort, and spending vast sums, is on the program to set up a system to destroy incoming ballistic missiles. The machinery is being built, and the money spent, even though there have been no realistic tests, many experts doubt that the system can work, and the threat against which it would supposedly defend—intercontinental missile attacks from major countries—is essentially nonexistent today.

At the same time, the US government wants to build

a new generation of nuclear weapons itself. One would be a "robust nuclear earth penetrator," to get at subterranean bunkers. If such a weapon penetrated eighty feet and had a one-kiloton explosion, the radioactive fallout would kill everyone on the surface within a radius of about half a mile.

In the face of official folly so great, most of us tend to turn off. The subject is too difficult, and too frightening. But Steven Weinberg does not turn off. He grapples with the danger and the folly in understandable and elegant prose.

During the cold war we had in Jerome Wiesner a scientist-writer who could convey the urgency of issues such as the Anti-Ballistic Missile Treaty with convincing clarity. Weinberg does the same at a time when the issues have become more obscure and when the American government is more resistant to scientific reasoning than were earlier conservative administrations.

Weinberg can make a point that had eluded us seem obvious. One example is that "as the world's leader in conventional weaponry, we have a very strong interest in preserving the taboo against the use or nuclear weapons."

He draws on history to explain why that is so. At the beginning of the twentieth century Britain's navy was dominant. Then it developed and built a new kind of battleship, the Dreadnought, that was vastly superior. Germany built its own and was able to compete without matching all of the British navy. Like Dreadnoughts, Weinberg says, nuclear weapons can act as equalizers between strong nations like the US "and weaker countries or even terrorist organizations."

He explores a crucial question: Why does the United States go on developing new nuclear weapons and antimissile defenses, at enormous and counterproductive cost? "As a scientist," he says, "I can recognize a kind of technological restlessness at work." There is pressure from the national weapons laboratories in Sandia and Los Alamos, New Mexico—and from Senator Pete Domenici of New Mexico. But those are not sufficient explanations. Weinberg adds one wonderful sentence: "There also seems to be a widespread sentiment in Congress and the public that it is inconsistent with American dignity to accept any limitations on our military technology."

Building new nuclear weapons systems is counterproductive in a fundamental sense that Weinberg sums up. We want to limit nuclear proliferation. But how can we be effective in persuading others to give up ultimate weapons if we insist on adding more to our enormous arsenal? We want rules that apply to everyone but us.

To pick out elements in Weinberg's analysis is really to mislead the reader into thinking that what he writes is forbidding to read. It is not. Steven Weinberg is that rarity, someone who really bridges the two cultures. He is a physicist who won the Nobel Prize. He is also at home in literature and history. Writing about weapons, he brings to his aid the Bayeux Tapestry, Shakespeare's *Henry V*, and the reason why fish swim in schools.

The American war in Iraq and its aftermath give special value to one of Weinberg's insights. Military organizations seek glory, he says, eschewing the more pedestrian work that may matter more. Thus the United States Army over the years after World War II gradually reduced its training in how to manage occupied countries.

The vainglory of individual commanders has become less of a danger with improved communications, Weinberg suggests. There is less chance of a Douglas MacArthur going off on his own on a dangerous escapade. "But there is a continuing danger from an institutionalized vainglory."

In many ways the United States has an admirable military today. Among other things it has dealt with the question of race more effectively than just about any other American institution. It is well trained and equipped. Its officers seem to me on the whole more sophisticated and more open-minded than the stereotype.

The problem lies in the political direction of our military, the choice of strategic weapons and of political targets for our great power. There is surely the risk of vainglory. And it is a problem peculiarly uncomfortable for a democracy. The choices are too complicated and dangerous, a president and his aides tell us; you must leave them to us. Steven Weinberg shows us why that cannot be.

—ANTHONY LEWIS

GLORY
AND
TERROR

As published in *The New York Review of Books*,
July 18, 2002

THE GROWING NUCLEAR DANGER

THE UNITED STATES POSSESSES AN ENORMOUS nuclear arsenal, left over from the days of the cold war. We have about 6,000 operationally deployed nuclear weapons,[1] of which roughly 2,000 are on intercontinental ballistic missiles, 3,500 on submarine-launched ballistic missiles, and a few hundred carried by bomber aircraft. These are thermonuclear weapons, considerably more powerful than the fission bombs that devastated Hiroshima and Nagasaki. Looking over these figures, one can hardly help asking, what are all these nuclear weapons for?

There was a rationale for maintaining a very large nuclear arsenal during the cold war: we had to be sure that the Soviets would be deterred from a surprise attack on the US by their certainty that enough of our arsenal would survive any such attack to allow us to deliver a devastating response. I don't say that US strategic requirements were actually calculated in this way, but the need for such a deterrent at least provided a rational argument for a large arsenal.

This rationale for a large nuclear arsenal is now obsolete. No country in the world could threaten our submarine-based deterrent, and even with an implausibly rapid development of nuclear weapons and missiles, for decades to come no country except Russia will be able to threaten more than a tiny fraction of our land-based deterrent.

Russia maintains a nuclear arsenal of a size similar to ours, though with a different mix of delivery vehicles. On May 24, 2002, Presidents Bush and Putin signed a treaty calling for a reduction in operationally deployed nuclear weapons on both sides to about 3,800 in 2007 and to about 1,700 to 2,200 in 2012. This treaty will almost certainly be ratified by the Senate; Democrats will generally be glad of any reduction in nuclear arms, and few Republicans will want to oppose President Bush on a matter of foreign relations. President Bush has said, "This treaty will liquidate the legacy of the cold war." But any celebration would be premature, for there is far less to this treaty than meets the eye.

For one thing, the rate of reduction is painfully slow. The START III agreement that was announced (though not signed or ratified) by Presidents Clinton and Yeltsin called for a reduction to about 2,000 to 2,500 "strategically deployed" nuclear weapons by 2007, not by the 2012 deadline of the Bush–Putin treaty. (The term "strategically deployed" differs from "operationally deployed" in including all weapons that are associated with delivery systems, whether or not they are actually ready to fire. Thus for instance the nuclear warheads of missiles on a submarine in dry-dock would be included on the list of strategically deployed weapons but not of operationally deployed weapons. When this difference is taken into account, the limit of 2,000 to 2,500

strategically deployed weapons in 2007 set by the START
III agreement is the same as the limit of 1,700 to 2,200
operationally deployed nuclear missiles in 2012 set by
the Bush–Putin treaty.) The treaty is highly reversible;
either party can withdraw with forty-five days' notice, and
unless renewed the treaty will expire in 2012. Also, unlike
former arms control agreements, the Bush–Putin treaty
would not call for the destruction of missiles or bombers,
only for the removal of their nuclear warheads or bombs.

Most important, the Bush administration has turned
back Russian efforts to require in this treaty that the
nuclear weapons withdrawn from deployed missiles
and bombers should be destroyed. The Defense Department's plans for nuclear weapons have been laid out in
a classified Nuclear Posture Review,[2] dated January 9,
2002, of which large sections were leaked a few months
later to the press.[3] The plans laid out in this review call
for the retention of about 7,000 intact warheads that
are not operationally deployed, not to mention a large

number of plutonium "pits" (the fission bomb that triggers a thermonuclear explosion) and other weapon components. Of course, the treaty does not call for the destruction of demobilized Russian nuclear weapons either, and it does not constrain Russian nuclear tactical weapons, so it actually increases the danger that some Russian weapons could fall into the hands of rogue states or terrorists. This treaty is not designed to "liquidate the legacy of the cold war," as President Bush claims, but to hold on to as much of that legacy as possible. Even taking into account the reductions called for by the Bush–Putin treaty, we are left still wondering what all these nuclear weapons are for.

There is one possible use of a large American nuclear arsenal: to launch a preemptive attack against Russian strategic weapons. I say "Russian," because the large size of our arsenal would be irrelevant for a preemptive attack against any other power. If we ever found that a hostile "rogue" state were about to deploy a few dozen nuclear-armed ICBMs, and if we could locate them, then they could be destroyed by only a tiny fraction of our nuclear arsenal, and in fact even by conventionally armed cruise missiles. On the other hand, even though we were unable to neutralize the Soviet deterrent during the cold war, now as Russian nuclear forces become increasingly immobile, with their missile-launching submarines tied up at dockside and their land-based mobile ICBMs kept in fixed garrisons, our large nuclear arsenal may put Russian nuclear forces at risk of being destroyed by a preemptive US strike. In the letter of transmittal of the Nuclear Posture Review to Congress, Secretary Rumsfeld said that "the US will no longer plan, size, or sustain its forces as though Russia presented merely a smaller version of the threat posed by the former Soviet Union." But that appears to be just what we are doing.

It might seem that the ability to launch a preemptive strike against Russian strategic nuclear forces is a good one to have, but in fact it poses enormous dangers, and to us as well as to Russia. The Russians can count missiles as well as we can, and as "prudent" defense planners they are likely to rate our chances of a successful preemptive attack more highly than we would. Even though they may understand that the US now has no plans for such a preemptive attack, they are bound to consider the possibility that this could change if relations between Russia and the US sour in future. This possibility is likely to seem more probable if the US proceeds with a national missile defense, which might be perceived to have some effectiveness against a ragged Russian second strike, or if we follow the recommendation of the Nuclear Posture Review that the US should develop real-time intelligence capabilities of a sort that would allow us to target even mobile Russian missiles on the road.

The danger is not that the Russians will get angry with us, or plan to attack us. The danger is that they will quietly adopt a cheap and easy defense against a pre-emptive American attack, by keeping their forces on a hair-trigger alert. This presents the US with the threat of a large-scale Russian attack by mistake during some future crisis; for instance, the Russians may receive misleading warnings of an imminent American attack and launch their own nuclear weapons before they can be destroyed on the ground. (According to Russian sources, it now takes fifteen seconds for the Russians to target their ICBMs, and then two to three minutes to carry out the launch.) This danger is exacerbated by the gradual decay of Russia's capabilities for surveillance of possible attacks and control of their own forces, a decay that has already led them on one occasion to mistake a Norwegian research rocket for an offensive missile launched from an American submarine in the Norwegian sea.[4]

For those who may think that this is a paranoid worry,

perhaps left over from cold war movies like *Fail Safe* or *Dr. Strangelove*, it is instructive to look back at mistakes made by American strategic forces during the Cuban missile crisis, the most dangerous crisis of the cold war[5]:

(1) On August 23, 1962, a navigational error led a B52 bomber on airborne alert—i.e., ready to retaliate if the US were attacked—which was supposed to be on a nonprovocative course heading over the Arctic Ocean toward Alaska, to head instead directly toward the Soviet Union. Its error was noticed when the bomber was only three hundred miles away from Soviet airspace. Despite this incident, and the well-known difficulties of navigation above the Arctic Circle, the routes of US bombers on airborne alert were not changed for months, not until after the October missile crisis. Luckily no similar navigational errors were made by our bombers during the missile crisis.

(2) On October 26, 1962, when US and Soviet forces

were already at a heightened state of alert, an intercontinental ballistic missile was launched from Vandenberg Air Force Base, as part of a test program that no one had thought to cancel. We do not know if the Soviets detected this launch, but they might have.

(3) The Cuban missile crisis happened to come at a time when new Minuteman I missiles were being installed at Malmstrom Air Force Base in Montana. In order to get these missiles ready for possible launch, Air Force and contractor personnel apparently bypassed safeguards that had been designed to prevent a launch by a single officer. Fortunately no officer decided to launch the missiles under his control.

We don't know what mistakes may have been made on the Soviet side. Whatever mistakes were made on either side did not lead to war, but this was evidently not because national leaders are able to completely control their forces under crisis conditions. As President Kennedy said during the Cuban missile crisis, "There is always some son-of-a-bitch who doesn't get the word."

Even though the threat of a large Russian mistaken attack is not acute, it is chronic. It is also the only threat we face that could destroy our country beyond our ability to recover. Compared with this threat, all other concerns about terrorism or rogue countries shrink into insignificance.

This brings me to the one real value of our large nuclear arsenal: we can trade away most of our arsenal for corresponding cuts in Russian forces. I don't mean cuts to about two thousand deployed weapons, but to not more than a few hundred deployed weapons on each side, and with each side having not more than a thousand nuclear weapons of all sorts, including those in various reserves, as called for by a 1997 report of the Committee on International Security and Arms Control of the National Academy of Sciences.[6] In that way, although the danger of a mistaken Russian launch would not be eliminated, the stakes would be millions or tens of millions of casualties, not hundreds of millions.

Such cuts would also reduce the danger that Russian nuclear weapons or weapons material could be diverted to criminals or terrorists. Instead of seeking the maximum future flexibility for both sides in strategic agreements with the Russians, we should be seeking the greatest possible irreversibility on both sides, based on binding ratified treaties. We ought also to be spending more on the program, originally sponsored by former Senator Sam Nunn and Senator Richard Lugar, that assists the Russians in controlling or destroying their excess nuclear materials. At this moment, when the Russians are eager to improve relations with the West, when considerations of economics provide them with a powerful incentive to reduce their nuclear forces, and when for the first time they have a president powerful enough to push such reductions through their military and political establishments, we have an unprecedented opportunity to begin to escape from the risk of nuclear annihilation. It is tragic that we are letting this opportunity slip away from us.

NOT ONLY ARE WE NOT MOVING FAST OR FAR ENOUGH in the right direction—in some respects the Bush administration seems to be moving in just the wrong directions. One example is the abrogation of the 1972 treaty limiting anti-ballistic missile systems.[7] Another example is the revival of the idea of developing nuclear weapons for use, rather than solely for deterrence.

For instance, the Nuclear Posture Review calls for the development of low-yield, earth-penetrating nuclear weapons for attacks on underground facilities, such as biological warfare laboratories in countries like Iraq. There are great technical difficulties here, which might prevent our using such a weapon even if we had it. When dropped from a bomber, our present earth-penetrating weapon, the B61-11, has penetrated only about ten feet into frozen tundra. The depth of penetration can be increased by accelerating the weapon down to the surface with a rocket; but increasing the velocity of impact beyond a certain point just causes the weapon to crumple, so that instead of the depth of penetration increasing, it decreases. Recent calculations show that an earth-penetrating weapon cannot be driven down to a depth greater than about four times its length in concrete.[8] This sets an upper limit on the depth of penetration of about eighty feet for a weapon that is twice the length of our B61-11. The actual depth that may be reached in practice may be considerably less, because the velocity of impact must be kept low enough to preserve the weapon's electrical circuits.

It is true that an eighty-foot depth is sufficient to put most of the energy of the explosion into a destructive underground blast wave, which can destroy facilities below the actual explosion, but even so, a one-kiloton explosion would only destroy tunnels that are at depths considerably less than three hundred feet, and not much more than that in a horizontal direction; the precise ranges are sensitive to geological details that we are not likely to know. An earth-penetrating nuclear weapon would be effective only against an underground target that is not too deep, and whose location is accurately known. To have confidence that the underground target had been destroyed we would have to have troops on the ground anyway, so that a missile attack might not even be necessary.

Even if an earth-penetrating nuclear weapon could destroy its target, we would be unlikely to use it because of radiation effects. In the 1950s a project known as Plowshare exploded a number of nuclear devices at various depths underground, with the hope of developing peaceful uses for nuclear explosions, like digging canals. Experience in these tests showed that to keep a nuclear explosion from breaking through the surface and spreading radioactive dirt into the atmosphere, a one-kiloton explosion would have to be kept below three hundred feet, with the depth required decreasing only slowly as the yield is decreased. (The penetration of a weapon through the earth would create a shaft to the surface, something that did not exist in the Plowshare tests, so the depth required to avoid fallout is bound to be even larger than indicated by these tests.) To avoid fallout from a nuclear explosion at a depth of only eighty feet it would be necessary to reduce the yield to nineteen tons of TNT, not much more than could be delivered using conventional explosives. I don't believe that there is any way for a nuclear weapon with a yield greater than a few tenths of a kiloton to penetrate to depths sufficient to avoid producing a great deal of radioactive fallout, without someone carrying it down in an elevator.

The fallout produced by a one-kiloton explosion at a depth of eighty feet would kill everyone on the surface within a radius of about half a mile. This estimate is for fallout under conditions of still air; wind could carry the fallout for tens of miles. We could be killing not only the local population, which (as in Afghanistan) we might be trying to enlist on our side, but also whatever forces we or our allies have on the ground.

There was another sign of increased interest in developing nuclear weapons for actual use in a recent statement by William Schneider, the chairman of the Defense Science Board. He announced a renewed study of nuclear-armed interceptor missiles as part of a system of missile defense. Nuclear-armed missile defense interceptors would have technical and political problems of their own, problems that have led to the abandonment of nuclear-armed interceptors as components in missile defense since the administration of Ronald Reagan.

For the dubious advantages of developing new nuclear weapons, we would pay a high price, including pressure for resumed testing of nuclear weapons. As I mentioned, calculations indicate that any nuclear weapon that would be effective against underground targets would release large quantities of radioactivity. Even if the depth of penetration of a nuclear weapon were somehow increased and the yield decreased enough so that no fallout was expected, how, without testing these weapons in action, could anyone ever have confidence that fallout would not escape, especially after the US weapon has created its own shaft to the surface? And how could anyone have confidence in a missile defense system based on nuclear-armed interceptors without tests that involve nuclear explosions in or above the atmosphere? We have not carried out even underground tests since the previous Bush administration. And, as is very much in our interest, neither has Russia or China.

The development of new nuclear weapons for warfighting would in itself violate our commitment under the 1970 Nuclear Nonproliferation Treaty to deemphasize the role of nuclear weapons and to work toward their total elimination. The resumption of nuclear testing for this purpose would make this violation concrete and dramatic, and would thereby gravely undermine the effectiveness of the Nonproliferation Treaty in discouraging nuclear weapons programs throughout the world.

A special danger of programs to develop nuclear weapons for use is that they may stand in the way of a really large-scale mutual reduction of nuclear arms. I'm not sure whether we are retaining a huge nuclear arsenal in order to facilitate such new weapons programs, or whether the weapons programs are being proposed in order to slow down cuts in our nuclear arsenal. Probably something of both. Back in the days when the first test ban treaty was being debated, one of the arguments against it was that it would stand in the way of Project Plowshare and also Project Orion, the development of a spacecraft propelled by nuclear explosions. (Both programs have long since been abandoned.) The development of nuclear weapons for attacking underground facilities or for missile defense may be today's Orion and Plowshare.

But the current proposals for new nuclear weapons are much more dangerous than the Plowshare or Orion programs. As the world's leader in conventional weaponry, we have a very strong interest in preserving the taboo against the use of nuclear weapons that has survived since 1945. Developing and testing new nuclear weapons for actual use rather than deterrence teaches the world a lesson that nuclear weapons are a good thing to have. This is not entirely a rational matter. I remember that once in the late 1960s I had lunch at MIT with the chief scientific adviser to the government of India. I asked about India's plans for developing and testing nuclear weapons, and he said that it all depended on whether the US and USSR could reach an agreement banning all future nuclear testing. I said that that seemed irrational, because it was not the US or the USSR that presented a military threat to India, and even if such a threat did develop, American and Soviet nuclear forces would in any case be so much greater than India's that it would not matter to India if the US or the USSR had stopped testing or gone on testing.

The Indian science adviser answered that politics is not always based on rational calculations, that there was great political dissension in Indian governing circles over whether to develop nuclear weapons, and that the spectacle of continued testing of nuclear weapons by the US or the USSR would strengthen the hands of those in India who favored developing nuclear weapons. Of course, the US and USSR did not stop testing at that time; India did develop nuclear weapons; and Pakistan followed suit. Is it likely that resumed US nuclear testing would have no effect on decisions about nuclear weapons in countries like Japan, or Egypt, or Germany? Is it likely that the Nonproliferation Treaty will survive when the US is developing and testing nuclear weapons for actual use?

After the signing of the Bush–Putin treaty, President

Bush was asked why it was necessary for us to keep two thousand nuclear weapons loaded on missiles. He answered that the future was uncertain. The same argument is often made to defend the development of new nuclear weapons. It is true that the future is uncertain, but where is it written that the way to reduce uncertainty is always to maximize our nuclear capabilities? We cannot tell what crisis may occur in US–Russian relations, a crisis that could put the US at risk from a mistaken launch on their part. We cannot tell what terrorists may take over or steal part of the Russian arsenal. We cannot tell what dangers we may face from a large Chinese arsenal, built to preserve their deterrent from the threat of an American first strike backed up by a missile defense system. We cannot tell what countries may be tipped toward a decision to develop nuclear weapons by new US weapons programs or resumed nuclear testing. There is no certainty whatever we do. We have to decide what are the most important dangers, and these dangers may be increased rather than decreased by other countries' responses to our own weapons programs. The Nuclear Posture Review strikingly fails to consider what other countries might do in response to our plans for nuclear weapons.

At the beginning of the twentieth century, Britain was overwhelmingly the world's greatest naval power, much as the US is today the world's leader in conventional arms. Then in 1905 Admiral Sir John Fisher, the First Sea Lord, pushed forward the construction of a new design for a fast battleship armed solely with twelve-inch guns, the biggest guns then available. The prototype was named after one of Nelson's ships, the *Dreadnought*. Dreadnoughts really were superior to all previous battleships, and suddenly what counted was not the size of a country's fleet, in which Britain was supreme, but the number of its Dreadnoughts. Other countries could now compete with Britain by building Dreadnoughts, and a naval arms race began between Britain and Germany, in which Britain would stay ahead only with great expense and difficulty. Admiral of the Fleet Sir Frederick Richards complained in Parliament that "the whole British fleet was morally scrapped and labeled obsolete at the moment when it was at the zenith of its efficiency and equal not to two but practically to all the other navies of the world combined."[9] Like Dreadnoughts, nuclear weapons can act as an equalizer between strong nations like the US, with great economic and conventional military power, and weaker countries or even terrorist organizations. It should be clear by now that national security is not always best served by building the best weapons.

As a scientist, I can recognize a kind of technological restlessness at work, from the building of the Dreadnought to this year's Nuclear Posture Review. Years before he pioneered the Dreadnought, as a newly appointed captain in charge of the Royal Navy's torpedo school, Fisher explained that "if you are a gunnery man, you must believe and teach that the world is saved by gunnery, and will only be saved by gunnery. If you are a torpedo man, you must lecture and teach the same thing about torpedoes." There is nothing corrupt or unpatriotic about such attitudes, but their consequences could be catastrophic.

—June 19, 2002

FOOTNOTES

1 The term "operationally deployed" refers to nuclear warheads that are installed on missiles ready to be fired plus bombs that are ready to be loaded on bombers in service.

2 Nuclear Posture Reviews are reports on US nuclear capabilities and plans requested by Congress from the Department of Defense. There have been just two of these reviews; the first was prepared during the Clinton administration. This article is based on my testimony at hearings on the latest Nuclear Posture Review held by the Senate Committee on Foreign Relations, May 16, 2002.

3 The contents of the Nuclear Posture Review were first reported by William Arkin in the *Los Angeles Times* on March 10, 2002. The leaked version is available at www.globalsecurity.org/wmd/library/policy/dod/npr.htm. There is also an unclassified briefing on the Nuclear Posture Review by J. D. Crouch, assistant secretary of defense for international security policy, available at www.defenselink.mil/news/Jan-2002/t01092002_t0109npr.html.

4 Apparently the Russians were informed in advance of the launch, but somehow this notice did not reach their strategic control center.

5 These examples are taken from Scott Sagan, *The Limits of Safety: Organizations, Accidents, and Nuclear Weapons* (Princeton University Press, 1993).

6 "The Future of US Nuclear Weapons Policy" (National Academy Press, 1997). More recently, a statement by Hans Bethe, Richard Garwin, Marvin Goldberger, Kurt Gottfried, Walter Kohn, and myself has called for an accelerating reduction of our nuclear arsenal and other steps to improve our security; see www.ucsusa.org.

7 For my comments on missile defense, see "Can Missile Defense Work?" in *The New York Review*, February 14, 2002.

8 Robert W. Nelson, "Low-Yield Earth-Penetrating Nuclear Weapons," *Science and Global Security*, Vol. 10, No. 1 (January 2002).

9 Quotes of Richards and Fisher are taken from Robert K. Massie, *Dreadnought: Britain, Germany, and the Coming of the Great War* (Ballantine, 1991).

As published in *The New York Review of Books*,
November 6, 2003

WHAT PRICE GLORY?

WAR OFFERS AMPLE OPPORTUNITIES FOR MOST varieties of foolishness. Among these, there is one sort of folly to which war is especially well suited: the lust for glory. One can hardly ever be sure about a commander's motives in any one case, but there are familiar signs of that lust: a readiness to accept a challenge to fight under unfavorable circumstances; a preference for taking action independent of allies or colleagues; an unreasoning predisposition for offense rather than defense; and an effort to seize a decisive role in winning victory. Examples come easily to mind. Antony accepted Agrippa's challenge to fight by sea at Actium, though he was stronger by land. In 1421 the Duke of Clarence violated the orders of his brother, King Henry V, and died attacking five thousand French troops with 150 mounted men-at-arms and no archers. To recapture the glory he had won by riding around

McClellan's army in search of its flank during the defense of Richmond in 1862, J. E. B. Stuart in June and July of 1863 led his cavalry on a wild ride through Maryland and Pennsylvania, even though it left the Army of Northern Virginia without the reconnaissance it needed in the week before the Battle of Gettysburg. Admiral William F. Halsey Jr. commanded the Third Fleet to chase Japanese battleships and carriers while other Japanese battleships threatened American soldiers landing on the beaches of Leyte Island.

Though there always will be soldiers and sailors "seeking the bubble reputation, even in the cannon's mouth," it seems that the vainglory of individual commanders has lately become less dangerous in war, as improvements in the technology of communications and surveillance have increased the ability of commanders to control subordinates. But there is a continuing danger from an institutionalized vainglory. Sometimes a branch of the military may try to maximize its opportunity for glory, turning its back on other less glamorous tasks that are really needed. This can become an ideology, like the French army's doctrine in 1914 of "*l'attaque à l'outrance.*" The military may even adopt weapons that serve more to enhance its glory than the likelihood of victory, and weapons themselves may become imbued with a glamour that stands in the way of sensible decisions about their use. One can find instances throughout history, and they extend unfortunately to the present day, with dangerous effects on our current defense policy.

ON FEBRUARY 1, 1917, GERMANY BEGAN A PROGRAM of unrestricted submarine warfare. The effect on British shipping was devastating. During the first three months German U-boats sank 844 ships, at a cost of only ten of their submarines. According to Winston Churchill, "That was, in my opinion, the gravest peril that we faced in all the ups and downs of that war."

It should have been obvious that the solution to the U-boat threat was to require merchant ships to sail in convoy. As Churchill later explained in *The World Crisis*,

> The size of the sea is so vast that the difference between the size of a convoy and the size of a single ship shrinks in comparison almost to insignificance. There was in fact nearly as good a chance of a convoy of forty ships in close order slipping

unperceived between the patrolling U-boats as there was for a single ship; and each time this happened, forty ships escaped instead of one.

(This is also the reason that fish of many species swim in schools.) Furthermore, forty merchant ships can be guarded by a much smaller number of destroyers or other escorts, while it would be impossible to send an escort with each merchant ship sailing alone. Even before sonar became available, a submerged submarine could be found when it attacked, by tracing back the track of the submarine's torpedo. It is true that a convoy presents a great many more targets than a single ship, but even with all those targets a single U-boat can destroy only a few ships before it exhausts its torpedoes or is destroyed or driven off by the escorts. U-boats in World War II learned to call in other U-boats to the attack when a convoy had been found by using radio to communicate with their headquarters in occupied France, but this technology was not available in World War I. (Nor is it available to fish.)

For several months after the start of unrestricted submarine warfare, while British ship losses mounted, the Admiralty continued to reject the use of convoys. For the Royal Navy in World War I, convoy duty was inglorious.[1] Arthur Marder, the leading historian of naval warfare in the early twentieth century, has explained in *From the Dreadnought to Scapa Flow* that

> the strange dogma had emerged in the pre-war generation that to provide warship escorts to merchant ships was to act essentially "defensively" (because it protected ships from attack), which was ipso facto bad, and that to use naval forces to patrol trade routes, however futile the result, was to act "offensively" against the warships of an enemy, and this was good.

In 1915 British Vice Admiral H. F. Oliver, chief of the War Staff, had explained to the secretary of the War

Cabinet, Sir Maurice Hankey, that the correct antidote to the U-boat menace was not convoy, but "hunting."

The trouble is that in the absence of long-range aviation and radar (and often even with them) it is very difficult for patrols to find submarines cruising in the open ocean. In the days when I used to work on antisubmarine warfare as a member of JASON, a group of academics serving as defense consultants, my efforts were mostly limited to solving equations, but in the early 1960s I did once go out on antisubmarine maneuvers. I was on a destroyer escort searching for a World War II diesel submarine that had left Key West that morning. Our ship and a destroyer searched all day, using passive and active sonar and magnetic detection devices, but it could not find the sub. At the end of the day the submarine had to send up a radio beacon to tell us where it was. Remembering this, when I later read the estimate of Rear Admiral William Sims (the American admiral in charge of US naval forces in Europe during World War I) that for patrols to find submarines, which can submerge at will, requires about one destroyer per square mile of ocean, I thought that Sims had been too optimistic. And of course there are a lot of square miles in the ocean. According to Sims's estimate, to find a submarine cruising somewhere in the western approaches to the British Isles would have required 25,000 destroyers.

As aggressive patrolling clearly failed to counter the U-boats and shipping losses grew, the Admiralty became desperate. When Sims arrived in London on April 10, 1917, he was invited to meet with the First Sea Lord, Admiral Sir John Jellicoe. Jellicoe told him that if shipping losses continued at their present rate Britain would have to leave the war, and that the Admiralty had no idea what to do about it. Sims cabled back to Washington that "briefly stated, I consider that at the present moment we are losing the war."

Pressure from Sims, Hankey, and Lloyd George finally forced the Admiralty to try using convoys. As an experiment, a convoy of merchant ships was sent from Gibraltar to Britain, and all ships arrived safely on May 20, 1917. The next day the Admiralty at last decreed that all merchant shipping to or from Britain must travel in convoys, and the rate of shipping losses dropped sharply.

In World War II it was the strategic air forces of Britain and the US that tried to play a glorious but unrealistic role—to win the war by themselves through strategic bombing, i.e., bombing aimed at the enemy's industry and population. There has been a great debate about the efficacy of strategic bombing in World War II. But however useful strategic bombing may have been, it could not have won the war by itself, at least not until the advent of nuclear weapons. In the invasion of Normandy it was surely necessary that all available bombers and their fighter escorts should come under Eisenhower's authority, so that he could divert them as needed from strategic bombing to support of ground troops and the interdiction of German reinforcements. Nevertheless,

James Doolittle and Arthur Harris, the commanders of the American Eighth Air Force and the British Bomber Command, put up a strong resistance to this arrangement, or to any pause in strategic bombing, and they managed to enlist Churchill's support.[2] To gain control over the strategic air forces during the critical phase of the invasion Eisenhower had to state that as long as he was in command he would accept no other arrangement, thus implicitly threatening to resign.

Even Stuart's failure to keep in touch with Lee before Gettysburg may have represented an institutionalized hubris rather than mere personal vainglory. Other Civil War cavalry generals also liked independent action. In August 1864 the commander of the Confederate Army of Tennessee, John B. Hood, sent his cavalry corps, under General Joseph Wheeler, to raid the railroad lines that were supplying Sherman's army in Georgia, with the expectation (according to Richard McMurry's book *Atlanta 1864*) that Wheeler would be gone for only a few days. As it happened, nobody in the Army of Tennessee would see Wheeler's troops again until mid-October. And in February 1864 the Union cavalry general Judson Kilpatrick talked Lincoln into allowing his cavalry to make a disastrous raid into Richmond in order to distribute pamphlets and free some prisoners. As Bruce Catton observed, "It was born of a romantic dream and it was aimed at glory, and glory was out of date."

We have recently had another example of the military distaste for unheroic roles. Just as the Royal Navy preferred "hunting" to convoy duty in World War I, and the Allied air forces preferred strategic bombing to ground support in World War II, and the cavalry preferred independent action to the support of infantry in the Civil War, so in recent years the United States Army has preferred to plan for fighting battles without worrying about how to govern conquered territory. The Army in World War II had an effective Division of Military Government. It was established in the Office of the Provost Marshall in July

1942, long before there were any captured Axis territories to govern. It was this division and the personnel whom it trained at the Charlottesville School of Military Government that made it possible for the United States later to govern Japan and parts of Germany and Italy in an orderly way, without encountering widespread looting, rioting, or guerrilla attacks.

In the years after the war, responsibility for military government was relocated in the Civil Affairs branch of the Army. Support for this branch was allowed to dwindle, and Civil Affairs survived several attempts to disband it as a separate unit, until in 1987 it finally found a home in the Special Operations Command. There it had to fight off attempts to divert its remaining funds and personnel slots to Special Forces. At the end of the 1980s, an Army-commissioned report, in a chapter called "Pruning Non-Essentials," asked the questions "Should 7,000 reservists continue to be trained to govern occupied nations? Is there a need for those trained in the administration of art, archives, and monuments to preserve the culture of occupied territories?"[3] Civil Affairs became known as a dead end for career officers.

There is now just one active-duty Civil Affairs unit, the 96th Civil Affairs Battalion (Airborne), headquartered at Fort Bragg; the remaining 95 percent of Civil Affairs personnel are reservists. In Afghanistan there are now only about two hundred Civil Affairs personnel, as compared with about 15,000 military government soldiers in the American Zone of Germany soon after the German surrender in World War II. A colonel (not in Civil Affairs) who is just back from Iraq tells me that there are about two thousand Civil Affairs officers there (not all in military government), leaving few anywhere else, and that although they are doing good work, there are not nearly enough of them. Unfortunately the Defense Department's priorities do not seem to have changed. Later this year it plans to close the ten-year-old Peacekeeping Institute of the Army War College.

3.

HISTORIES OF MILITARY TECHNOLOGY OFTEN DESCRIBE how the adoption of newly developed weapons is delayed by cultural influences. (Perhaps the most striking example was the refusal of the Tokugawa shoguns to allow guns in Japan.) But in these histories, when new weapons are finally adopted, it is always because of their objective effectiveness, rather than something as irrational as a lust for glory.

In his influential 1962 book *Medieval Technology and Social Change*, the distinguished medieval historian Lynn White follows this pattern. As an example of new military technology, he chose the combination of stirrup and lance. The foot-stirrup was unknown in classical antiquity. As White tells the story, it was invented in China sometime around the fifth century AD. Nomadic horsemen brought the stirrup through Central Asia to Constantinople. Nowhere along this journey did it have much effect on how battles were fought. But when the stirrup reached Western Europe late in the seventh century its effect was explosive. The stirrup allowed a horseman with "couched" lance, i.e., one held between the body and the upper arm, to deliver the whole force of a charging horse at the tip of his lance, without losing his seat. White argued that suddenly it was necessary to recruit horsemen who could afford the armor and war horses needed to fight in this way, horsemen who could only be paid by the grant of lands. Starting in 732, Charles Martel, the great mayor of the palace of Merovingian France, began to seize church lands and grant them to his cavalry. A new class of feudal knights and nobles was born.[4]

I have my doubts about this story. There is no question that stirrups are a good thing, as everyone knows who has ever tried to get on a horse. I don't doubt that the cavalry charge with couched lance became a popular tactic after 1100. But was it adopted because it was effective?

The use of the stirrup that White thought was "above

all" important in tipping the balance in favor of cavalry over infantry, enabling a mounted knight to charge with couched lance, which is also the one tactic in which the stirrup is indispensable, does not seem to have been very effective against infantry. In such a charge each knight can only kill one foot soldier before a general melee begins in which the lance is useless. A "destrier," a horse strong enough to carry an armored knight and bred and trained to charge an enemy, was enormously expensive. As the Chorus says in *King Henry the Fifth*, "they sell the pasture now to buy the horse." When we consider also the cost of the knight's and horse's armor, and of the necessary grooms and remounts, killing a foot soldier this way seems to have been hardly cost-effective. It would be like tanks without guns attacking infantry by running them down, one by one. Doubtless the tanks would defeat an equal number of foot soldiers, but in a war between two countries with equal resources, the side that used its resources this way would surely lose.

Also, foot soldiers were not defenseless in the Middle Ages. They could stand behind pointed stakes set in the ground, as the English archers did at Agincourt and other battles of the Hundred Years' War. They could protect themselves with long pikes, as Italian foot soldiers did to repulse the cavalry of Emperor Frederick I at Legnano in 1176, or fight on marshy ground, as Flemish pikemen did in repulsing the French cavalry at Courtrai in 1302, or on hilly ground, as the Swiss did in defeating Leopold of Austria at Morgarten in 1315. And the foot soldiers could fight back with missile weapons. A bolt from a crossbow or an arrow from a long bow could penetrate all but the best armor. It was English archers who defeated the French knights at Crécy, Poitiers, and Agincourt.

I do not know of a single European battle in the Middle Ages that was won by a charge of cavalry with couched lances against a line of foot soldiers. No clear examples are mentioned by Charles Oman in his classic two-volume *A History of the Art of War in the Middle Ages*. Granted, foot soldiers all but disappeared from European battlefields in the high Middle Ages, from 1100 to 1300, but apparently not because they had been defeated by the lance and stirrup.[5]

Oddly, White mentions only one European battle to prove the superiority of the new military technology, the Battle of Hastings on October 14, 1066. It is true that the Normans under Duke William were mostly mounted at Hastings, and they defeated King Harold's English army, which fought on foot. But the English soldiers were probably outnumbered by the Normans, and they were exhausted. After defeating an invasion by a Norwegian army under Harald Hardraade at Stamford Bridge on September 25, they had arrived in London on October 6, having marched the two hundred miles from York, and they then marched another fifty-eight miles to the neighborhood of Hastings. What is more, it is not clear that the Norman cavalry at Hastings ever charged English foot soldiers with couched lance.[6] The only reliable testimony to the weapons used at Hastings is the Bayeux tapestry, embroidered not long after the battle.[7] Looking over reproductions of the whole tapestry, I see plenty of lances in the hands of Norman cavalry, but that proves nothing. Lances had been widely used by cavalry for stabbing and throwing since long before the invention either of stirrups or feudalism. Many of the lances shown in the Bayeux tapestry are held above the head, as if they are about to be thrown.

Just one panel, number 65, shows what may be a couched lance being used to attack an English foot soldier, but there is no way to tell if this is the result of a cavalry charge. I find it telling that none of the lances shown on the Bayeux tapestry have the kind of handhold (such as the conical handholds known as vamplates that are shown on later illustrations of tournaments) that would allow a knight on a charging horse to drive the lance into an enemy. Without such a handle, a lance striking anything would just slide through the knight's armpit, stirrups or no stirrups. In any case, the English were defeated at Hastings more by Norman archers than by knights. The Bayeux tapestry shows an Englishman, generally believed to be Harold, struck in the eye by an arrow.

So if the cavalry charge with couched lance was an ineffective tactic against infantry, why did the lance become the standard weapon of medieval cavalry, and why did cavalry dominate the battlefields of the high Middle Ages? It seems likely to me that, instead of the new class of feudal nobility being called into being to take advantage of the combination of stirrup and couched lance, feudalism arose for other reasons,[8] and the cavalry charge with couched lance became the favorite tactic of the feudal knights and nobles because it gratified their desire for military glory. Landowners could see themselves as military heroes, not merely as recruiting sergeants of the prince. The great expense of this tactic was an advantage, not a drawback, because peasants could not afford a destrier and armor. The reason that foot soldiers were not used in battle is not that they would have been ineffective, but that they were common. If this all sounds too illogical to be true, recall Oman's verdict on the knights of the high Middle Ages: "A feudal force presented an assemblage of unsoldierlike qualities such as have seldom been known to coexist."

The cavalry charge with couched lance found its real use in tournaments. These gorgeous rituals gave skillful knights like England's William Marshall the opportunity to become international celebrities. It is sometimes said that tournaments became popular in the twelfth century as training grounds for real battle,[9] but it may be equally true to say that cavalry battles with infantry excluded served as training grounds for tournaments.

4.

IT IS NOT HARD TO FIND EXAMPLES CLOSER to the present of weapons that were adopted more for glory than for military effectiveness. Between the world wars, officers of the US Army Air Corps imagined that land-based aircraft would not only be able to destroy the enemy's industry by strategic bombing, but would also be able to conquer enemy fleets. Air Corps General William Mitchell predicted that air power "will not only dominate the land but the sea as well." Just as medieval knights were supposed to make plebeian foot soldiers unnecessary, bombers would make navies irrelevant.

For bombers to act independently at sea beyond coastal waters without having to be carried to the attack by naval vessels, they would have to have a very long range and carry a large bomb load, just as they would for strategic bombing. Such an airplane would have to be large, so it could not be used as a dive bomber, and it would therefore have to release its bombs in level flight. To avoid antiaircraft fire it would have to bomb from a high altitude. After a competition among several aircraft manufacturers, the Boeing Corporation in January 1936 received a contract for a bomber to meet these requirements. It would eventually be named the B17, or "Flying Fortress," and after the war it would become the glamorous star of the movies *Memphis Belle* and *Twelve O'Clock High*.

The B17 met all technical specifications of the Department of the Army, but it could not fulfill the purposes for which it was planned. After the attack on Pearl Harbor, B17s were sent to Midway Island. As a Japanese fleet approached Midway in June 1942, it was spotted by B17s. In fifty-five sorties between June 3 and 5, the B17s dropped 315 bombs, but despite optimistic reports from the pilots, not a single one of these bombs struck a Japanese ship. Antiaircraft fire from the Japanese fleet kept the B17s above 20,000 feet, and at that altitude it was just too hard to drop a bomb on a target as small as a ship. Also, like medieval foot soldiers dodging an attack by knights with couched lances, ships can maneuver out of the way of bombs dropped from high altitude. As Samuel Eliot Morison remarked, in his *History of United States Naval Operations in World War II*, the B17s would have done more damage by tracking the Japanese ships than by trying to bomb them, but their pilots were trained only for bombing.

The confidence of the Army Air Force in its ability to bomb enemy ships arose in part from a dramatic demonstration staged in 1921 by Mitchell, in which Army bombers had successfully sunk a number of surrendered German warships, including the dreadnought *Ostfriesland*. But the German ships were at anchor, not maneuvering, and since they were not firing at the aircraft, it was safe to bomb them from low altitude. The four Japanese carriers at Midway were sunk not by B17s but by short-range Navy SBD dive bombers, which had been carried to the battle by the *Enterprise* and *Hornet*. During 1943, B17s were mostly withdrawn from the Pacific theater, though a few were kept for less showy activities like dropping life rafts to shipwrecked sailors.

The B17 also encountered trouble even in its primary role of strategic bombing. To have any chance of hitting targets like factories and railroad marshaling yards without our present satellite-based global positioning system, bombers had to attack in daylight. But flying over enemy territory in daylight made them vulnerable to attack by enemy interceptor airplanes as well as anti-aircraft artillery. For this reason the design of the B17 had sacrificed part of its bomb capacity to enable it to carry exceptionally heavy armament: thirteen machine guns, manned by six crew members. (The maximum bomb load of the B17 was less than that of the British Lancaster[10] or the American B24. The B24 proved more useful than the B17, but it never attracted the same public attention.) The Air Force expected that B17s flying in tight formation would be able to fight off interceptors by themselves and reach targets beyond the range of American fighter escorts. Experience did not bear this out. In a daylight raid on August 17, 1943, a force of 315 unescorted B17s attacked a ball-bearing factory at Schweinfurt and a Messerschmitt factory at Regensburg, and lost sixty bombers and their precious crews. At that rate of loss, the Eighth Air Force could not have continued daylight strategic bombing for more than a few more raids without losing almost all of its strength. Daylight strategic bombing deep into Germany had to be suspended, until long-range escort fighters like the P51 became available in February–March 1944.

Despite all disappointments about the ineffectiveness of the B17 in performing the tasks for which it had been planned, it embodied the dreams of glory of the Air Force, and became a symbol of American air power. Over 12,000 B17s were built during the war, along with other bombers. It is true that B17s along with other bombers did take an important part in the war by attacking German synthetic oil plants and transportation facilities after long-range escorts became available, and above all in forcing Germany to divert artillery and fighter aircraft from battlefields to air defense. But the huge commitment of American resources to the B17 limited other production. Allied war planning was continually constrained by a shortage of landing craft, but never by a shortage of B17s.

5.

SINCE WORLD WAR II IT HAS BEEN ROCKETS and nuclear weapons that have the glamour that used to surround bombers or lances. There is no doubt about the extraordinary effectiveness of modern high-technology weapons in certain circumstances. But it always needs to be asked at which tasks are they effective, and which of these tasks actually need to be accomplished?

In the decades since nuclear weapons were used in war, there has developed a healthy conviction that these weapons should not be used again for anything but deterrence. In a remarkable international bargain, a number of countries agreed in 1970 that they would not develop nuclear weapons at all, in exchange for a pledge by the US and other nuclear powers to de-emphasize the role of nuclear weapons and to work toward their elimination. Now the Bush administration has turned its back on the Non-Proliferation Treaty by calling for work on a new generation of low-yield nuclear weapons. This would add nothing to our nuclear deterrent, but might actually be used in fighting wars. Prominent in the administration's wish list is a "robust nuclear earth penetrator," a nuclear weapon that could penetrate into the earth to attack subterranean bunkers and laboratories.

The political pressure for these developments comes in part from the national weapons laboratories, especially Sandia and Los Alamos, whose leaders would like to return to the glory days of designing and testing new nuclear weapons. (The weapons labs are powerfully aided by Senator Pete Domenici, the chairman of the subcommittee that deals with appropriations for nuclear programs. Domenici represents New Mexico, where Sandia and Los Alamos are located.) The earth penetrator is also actively supported by the Air Force, which would drop it. There also seems to be a widespread sentiment in Congress and the public that it is inconsistent with American dignity to accept any limitations on our military technology.

As with the couched lance, it is hard to think of a plausible mission in which new low-yield nuclear weapons would actually be effective. As I have discussed previously in these pages,[11] a nuclear weapon carried underground by a robust earth penetrator would only be able to attack targets that are not buried too deeply and whose location is precisely known, and any such attack would inevitably produce large quantities of radioactive fallout at the surface, possibly killing large numbers of civilians.

The problem is not so much that the money spent on new nuclear weapons would be wasted. The cost of these programs is in the range of tens or hundreds of millions rather than billions of dollars. The problem is, rather, that the United States would be violating the 1970 Non-Proliferation Treaty and encouraging a new round of nuclear weapons development throughout the world. For a nation with an enormous lead over the rest of the world in nonnuclear military technology, this would be foolishness on a scale that even medieval knights might find implausible.

It was to avert such dangers that Congress in 1993 passed the Spratt-Furst Amendment to the 1994 National Defense Authorization Act. This amendment stated that it was not the policy of the United States to develop or use nuclear weapons of low yield, defined as less than the equivalent of five thousand tons of TNT. There has been an argument within Congress and the Department of Energy about whether the Spratt-Furst Amendment bans research as well as development of such weapons, but this argument may become moot. In a message from the Office of Management and Budget to the House Armed Services Committee in May of this year, the administration called for a complete repeal of the Spratt-Furst Amendment. The Senate has voted to repeal the amendment, but at the time of writing the House has not. The issue will presumably be settled in a House-Senate conference committee this autumn.

National missile defense has for some the allure of a good science fiction movie. A fleet of American satellites detects the launch of a missile by some evil regime in Asia. Powerful radars in Alaska track the missile's warhead, and American missiles are launched to meet it above the earth's atmosphere. Our missiles then release exo-atmospheric kill vehicles (EKVs), which guide themselves to collide with the enemy warhead, and destroy the bomb it contains. Seattle is saved.

Unfortunately, missile defense is not likely to work so neatly.[12] So far, tests of the EKV have alternated between successes and failures, and now the tests have been suspended while work continues on the booster that would carry the EKVs into space. But even if the tests had an unbroken series of successes, they would still have the same quality of phoniness as the destruction of the Ostfriesland by bombers in 1921. It is not that tests like this have no value, but rather that they can't be relied on to tell us whether the system being tested would be really effective. Just as the *Ostfriesland* in Mitchell's test was neither maneuvering nor shooting at the bombers attacking it, none of the warheads targeted in the tests of the EKV has been accompanied by the simple realistic decoys that could defeat the EKVs. Nor have other possible countermeasures against EKVs been addressed in any of the tests so far. In the real world B17s could not hit Japanese warships that were maneuvering in unpredictable ways, and similarly our EKVs will not be able to destroy incoming warheads if the enemy uses countermeasures that we cannot know in advance.

The proponents of missile defense to whom I have talked generally acknowledge these problems, but they argue that we must at least make a start, and then learn as we go along. As Secretary Rumsfeld has put it, the proposed national missile defense system is at least better than nothing. I think a strong case can be made that it is worse than nothing. It will hurt relations with our allies, discourage Russia from taking its missiles off ready alert, and encourage China to increase its missile forces more than had been planned.

A "boost-phase intercept" system, which relies on attacking missile boosters soon after launch, would not be subject to these criticisms if it defended our allies as well as ourselves, and if it were located so that it could not reach missiles launched from Russia or China. But a recent study by a panel of the American Physical Society indicates that feasible interceptors would not be able to reach missiles launched from North Korea or Iran before warheads separate from the booster.[13]

Granted, one cannot be sure about how other countries will respond to an American missile defense system. But there is no question about the enormous cost of missile defense. We are currently spending about nine billion dollars a year just for research and development, and a deployed system covering the entire United States would surely cost several hundred billion dollars, all to ineffectively counter a highly implausible threat. Any missile attack on the US would immediately reveal which country launched it and expose it to devastating retaliation. Such deterrence protected the US from nuclear attack for almost half a century of cold war. It is true that without missile defense the US might be deterred from trying to overthrow a "rogue state" that possessed nuclear-armed intercontinental missiles. But for the US to take such an action without fear of nuclear retaliation, a missile defense system would have to be nearly perfect, not merely better than nothing.

Even those for whom national defense is the one clearly legitimate reason for government spending ought to consider whether the enormous sums required for missile defense would not be better spent on defense of other sorts. There are many ways to attack the United States with nuclear or biological weapons that, unlike ballistic missiles, do not immediately reveal the source of the attack. Over the past year or so I have served on two panels of the Council on Foreign Relations, the Hart-Rudman Independent Task Force on Homeland Security Imperatives and the Rudman Independent Task Force on Emergency Responders. It has been painful to learn how much the lack of funds has limited our ability to defend the country from terrorists. For instance, the cost of adequate physical security at our commercial seaports would be about \$2 billion, but only \$92.3 million in federal grants has been authorized and approved. The US may be spending one third of what is required to adequately provide for those who would have to respond to emergencies. American cities have fewer policemen and firemen now than they did before September 11, 2001. Last October the Hart-Rudman panel concluded that "a year after September 11, 2001, America remains dangerously unprepared to prevent and respond to a catastrophic attack on US soil." This remains true.

We face another danger, even greater than that from terrorists. For all the good relations between Russia and the US today, Russian nuclear forces are frozen in a cold war configuration, one designed to respond to warning of an American attack within ten minutes by a massive nuclear counterattack, before a single nuclear weapon can reach Russia's land-based missiles or control centers. This puts not just a city or two but the entire US in danger of irreversible destruction by mistake, a danger that will increase as Russia's capacities to detect an attack become more and more degraded. Much could be done to lessen this danger, such as seriously reducing nuclear arsenals on both sides and sharing information about missile launches, but this has not been a priority of any US administration. Reducing the threat of nuclear attack by mistake, improving port security, providing for emergency responses, bringing effective government to Iraq and Afghanistan—in none of these do our leaders find sufficient glory.

—October 7, 2003

STEVEN WEINBERG

FOOTNOTES

1 To be fair, more sensible arguments were offered against convoys. It was said that merchant ships could not sail in tight formations, but when they tried it turned out that they could. It was said that there were not enough convoy escorts, but it turned out that the destroyers available could do the job.

2 Eisenhower in *Crusade in Europe* says that it was Doolittle, Harris, and Churchill that opposed giving him authority over the strategic air forces during the invasion, while Gerhard Weinberg's history of World War II, *A World at Arms*, attributes the opposition also to Ira Eaker, the commander of the Fifteenth Air Force in Italy, as well as to Doolittle and Harris. Russell Weigley in *Eisenhower's Lieutenants* cites only Harris as resisting Eisenhower's authority. If Weigley is right, then British national pride as well as air force vainglory may have played a role in this dispute.

3 Stanley Sandler, *Glad to See Them Come and Sorry to See Them Go: A History of US Army Civil Affairs and Military Government, 1775–1991* (USASOC, 1998), p. 372.

4 Michael Howard endorses this account in *War in European History*.

5 Oman mentions two battles that encouraged the nobility after the revival of infantry in the fourteenth century to believe in the continued superiority of cavalry over infantry: Mons-en-Pevele in 1304 and Cassel in 1328. As pointed out recently by Kelly DeVries in *Infantry Warfare in the Early Fourteenth Century*, though French cavalry did defeat Flemish infantry in both battles, this was only after the Flemings had become disorganized by ill-conceived charges against the French. At Mons-en-Pevele an initial French cavalry charge was turned back by the Flemish infantry, and at Cassel the French did not even try to attack the Flemish line until after the Flemish attack.

6 White does not say in so many words that the Normans charged the English with couched lances at Hastings, but he refers to Hastings as the "most spectacular" application of the new military technology, and as "a conflict between the military methods of the seventh century and those of the eleventh century."

7 There are no eyewitness written accounts of the Battle of Hastings. The most frequently quoted contemporary accounts are *The Deeds of William*, by the Duke's chaplain, William of Poitiers, and *The Song of the Battle of Hastings*, attributed to Guy, Bishop of Amiens. They mostly mention arrows, javelins, and swords. There are a few places where English translations refer to lances (none of them appearing at the same point of the battle in both accounts), but it is not always clear that this is what was meant in the Latin originals. The Latin word *hasta* can mean either lance or spear. Also, nowhere in either account is it clear that an attack was make with the lance couched. The translators of William of Poitiers comment that the use of the couched lance was restricted in this battle, because of the hilly terrain.

8 For instance, according to the much-debated thesis of Henri Pirenne, it was the closing of the Mediterranean to European trade by the Arabs that was responsible for the replacement of Roman civilization in the West with feudalism.

9 Wellington is supposed to have remarked that the Battle of Waterloo was won on the playing fields of Eton. But, being smarter than medieval generals, he knew better than to arm his soldiers with cricket bats.

10 The Royal Air Force had been even more enthusiastic about strategic bombing than the US Army Air Force, but they were more realistic about the ability of bombers to defend themselves. They gave up the goal of precision bombing and attacked German cities at night, hoping to weaken Germany by damaging morale and workers' housing.

11 "The Growing Nuclear Danger," pp. 2–29.

12 I discussed this in more detail in "Can Missile Defense Work?," *The New York Review*, February 14, 2002.

13 "Report of the American Physical Society Study Group on Boost-Phase Intercept Systems for National Missile Defense," July 2003, available at www.aps.org. Although President Bush on December 17, 2002, announced a "layered" national missile defense, with boost-phase intercept as the first line of defense, this intercept phase has been eliminated since then as a component of defense against intercontinental ballistic missiles.

STEVEN WEINBERG

BOOKS DRAWN ON FOR THIS ESSAY

A Stillness at Appomattox:
The Army of the Potomac, Vol. 3
by Bruce Catton.
Anchor, 438 pp., $14.95 (paper)

The World Crisis, Vol. 4
by Winston S. Churchill.
Scribner, 322 pp.
(1964; out of print)

Infantry Warfare in the Early
Fourteenth Century
by Kelly DeVries.
Boydell and Brewer (distributed
in the US by University of
Rochester Press),
216 pp., $29.95

Crusade in Europe
by Dwight D. Eisenhower.
Johns Hopkins University Press,
608 pp., $19.95 (paper)

The Carmen de Hastingae Proelio of
Guy, Bishop of Amiens
translated and edited by
Catherine Morton and
Hope Muntz.
Clarendon Press, 149 pp.
(1972; out of print)

War in European History
by Michael Howard.
Oxford University Press,
175 pp., $15.95 (paper)

From the Dreadnought
to Scapa Flow, Vol. 4
by Arthur J. Marder.
Oxford University Press, 364 pp.
(1969; out of print)

Atlanta 1864:
Last Chance for the Confederacy
by Richard M. McMurry.
University of Nebraska Press,
229 pp., $35.00

Winged Defense:
The Development and Possibilities
of Modern Air Power—Economic
and Military
by William Mitchell.
Dover, 320 pp.
(1988; out of print)

Coral Sea, Midway, and Submarine
Actions, May 1942–August 1942
by Samuel Eliot Morison.
Book Sales, 307 pp., $6.50
(paper)

*A History of the Art of War
in the Middle Ages*
by C. W. C. Oman.
Burt Franklin, two volumes
(1924; out of print)

*The Art of War in the Middle Ages,
AD 378–1515*
by C. W. C. Oman, revised and
edited by John H. Beeler.
Cornell University Press,
176 pp., $13.50 (paper)

Mohammed and Charlemagne
by Henri Pirenne.
Dover, 304 pp., $12.95 (paper)

*Hankey: Man of Secrets, Vol. 1,
1877–1918*
by Stephen Roskill.
Naval Institute Press, 672 pp.
(1970; out of print)

The Victory at Sea
by William S. Sims.
James Stevenson, 428 pp.,
$25.95 (paper)

*The Bayeux Tapestry:
A Comprehensive Survey*
edited by Frank Stenton.
Phaidon, 182 pp.
(1957; out of print)

*Eisenhower's Lieutenants:
The Campaign of France and Germany,
1944–1945*
by Russell F. Weigley.
Indiana University Press, 822
pp., $30.95

*A World at Arms:
A Global History of World War II*
by Gerhard L. Weinberg.
Cambridge University Press,
1,198 pp., $45.00

*Medieval Technology
and Social Change*
by Lynn White.
Oxford University Press,
216 pp., $13.95 (paper)

*The Gesta Guillelmi of
William of Poitiers*
translated and edited by
R. H. C. Davis and
Marjorie Chibnall.
Oxford University Press,
248 pp., $92.50

The New York Review of Books

The New York Review of Books, published twenty times each year, has been called "the country's most successful intellectual journal." (*The New York Times*)

To find out more, including how to subscribe, visit our website: www.nybooks.com. Or call or write:

The New York Review of Books
1755 Broadway
New York, New York 10019
Telephone: (212) 757-8070
Fax: (212) 333-5374
Email: nyrsub@nybooks.com